I AM

Smiling Again

A Journey to Overcoming Sexual Assault

By The Girl Next Door™

I AM Smiling Again:

A Journey to Overcoming Sexual Assault

By: The Girl Next Door™

Contents

WHO IS THE GIRL NEXT DOOR™?

Welcome! You may already know her but be patient with her as she introduces herself to the new reader joining her on this journey. After all, she is just a girl that lives next door to you. If you already know her, feel free to skip to the introduction. This journey will be a peaceful one.

It was June 2021. She had traveled internationally, including on all seven continents. After being locked in due to the pandemic, she needed a trip. It could have been a trip anywhere. She just needed to getaway. She decided to rent an Airbnb in Salt Lake City, Utah, for two weeks.

She made sure her Abyssinian guinea pig, Lionhead rabbit, and Maine Coon cat had plenty of supplies to be self-sufficient in her absence. Then she went on her road trip.

She would check the security camera at her house once a day. Halfway through her trip, something interesting happened. Even though she was in a different state, with a different time zone, she checked her security camera exactly when a police officer came to her door. Not wanting to impede law enforcement, she called the non-emergency line to inquire about what was going on.

The dispatcher said the officer was doing a wellness check. "On whom?" she asked. The officer is checking up on ... ...you. Why would a police officer need to check on her? The dispatcher stated her garage door had been open for a few days and many concerned neighbors called to ask for a wellness check. The neighbors didn't know her name, so they kept calling her the same thing. "It is not like The Girl Next Door™ to expose all her things in her garage," one neighbor after another stated. She confirmed she was alright and asked if the police officer could close the garage door, so she wouldn't have to shorten her trip.

Even though She knew it wasn't in his job description, she watched, on her security camera, as the police officer quickly closed the garage door. She thanked the dispatcher and police officer for saving her trip, and The Girl Next Door™ had been officially named.

She fits the stereotypical prototype.

- Shy
- Modest
- Intelligent
- sweet-natured
- reserved
- modest
- predictable
- reliable
- wholesome
- introverted
- lowkey
- humble

The Girl Next Door™ has traditional values. She would never intentionally hurt others. She is honest, independent, loyal, Godfearing, and kindhearted. She is admired from afar. People find her intimidating to approach, although she doesn't understand why. She is special, but it is hard for her to believe it.

Growing up, she is your BFF (best friend forever). Yes, the school bullies would take her dessert at lunchtime. She was picked on for no other reason than having a pleasant, sweet personality. She has integrity, and no one can buy her love.

The Girl Next Door™ is naturally pretty but can't see it. She dresses modestly for comfort, but she can get all fancied up when she gets to go out. Because of her humble beginnings, she is low maintenance. She can do her hair, nails, and make-up. She is rare because she is real. She is just trying to be herself, so she doesn't wear fake lashes, nails, or hair.

The Girl Next Door™ is beautiful on the inside and outside. She prefers to be in the background so you can shine. Now she wants to help you. She is not on any social media platform, so you can't send her a direct message. She can be counted on to give good advice. The Girl Next Door™ tries not to gossip or share your secrets. You can talk to her for hours because she is safe. She will not let you ever give up. During this self-love trip, she wants to convey that you can overcome sexual assault. If this journey helps you, share it and help someone else. Taking this journey with you is usually tricky because she must come out of her comfort zone to help you. She wants to be by your side as you take this self-love journey. She wants to be by your side as you take this self-love journey. This is one of the saddest and darkest journeys yet, so take breaks whenever you need to and return. If you are too triggered, take a break and return when you can. It is okay. It is alright. You got this. We must start somewhere. We might as well begin now.

First, I want you to know that **<u>no one</u>** can tell by simply looking at you. You are beautiful. You have always been beautiful to me, but that is another journey.

As we have a light conversation in passing, I see you sometimes from my window. I have noticed the spark in your eyes has dimmed. You are neglecting your looks and hygiene. You seem depressed. You have compromised your health by gaining or losing a lot of weight. You are isolating yourself more. You seem uneasy in everyday social situations when I watch you from afar. I wanted to talk to you about it, but I don't want to infringe on your privacy or have you re-experience the trauma by sharing it with me.

You are trying to be strong to make it through whatever. I want to help you with the guilt, shame, anger, and powerlessness you may be experiencing.

I want to see you smile again.

INTRODUCTION

When did you lose your smile? For some, it was when they were a toddler, a child, a teenager, a young adult, or some other time during their life.

This journey is gender neutral because both girls and boys, men and women, experience sexual assault.

During the trip to Salt Lake City, Utah, their NBA basketball team made it to the playoffs. The Girl Next Door™ was fortunate enough to get a ticket behind their team's bench. To the fan's disappointment, the team lost in the game's first half. At half-time, the team gave The Girl Next Door™ a happy birthday shoutout on the jumbotron. During half-time, the basketball team learned from their mistakes and developed a strategy to implement, which caused them to go on and win the playoff game.

The real-life application here is even if the first half is over and you are losing, you can regroup at half-time, learn from tragedy and go on to have the most beautiful, productive, fantastic life.

Sexual assault is a term that refers to nonconsensual fondling or unwanted sexual touching. It is when a person forces to orally penetrate a sex organ of another person without the consent of the victim. It can occur when a person's body is penetrated via the vagina or anus. Rape is a form of sexual assault; however, not all sexual assault is rape.

Throughout this journey, all sexual assault victims are considered innocent survivors. Despite the specific circumstances behind each sexual assault, the most crucial step to being able to smile again is to acknowledge you are an innocent survivor. You have been blaming yourself for far too long. As an innocent survivor, you have no choice but to accept what has happened and take the appropriate legal actions, if possible.

You will have to strengthen yourself daily with people and resources contributing to the healing process. Until you are smiling again, you may have to temporarily stay away from everyone that is not in agreement with accepting you as an innocent survivor. Sometimes others are incapable of understanding the level of trauma you have experienced. They may not even believe it occurred.

Can a human composed of a body, soul, and spirit overcome sexual assault? When the body is violated, a part of the soul is destroyed, but the spirit is never touched. This results in lifelong trauma. Managing this trauma is crucial to getting your smile back and having healthy acquaintances, friendships, and relationships.

This journey to overcoming sexual assault is a lifelong process. This journey we will take together is unique from anything you have tried before and can be used to supplement help from counselors, therapists, life coaches, psychiatrists, or other professionals.

Due to the nature of this topic, self-care is imperative. Take a break from our journey as often as needed, and then return when you are ready. It is reasonable to cry or even scream, if necessary, to release some of the pain. You may have to work out as a release or get a spa treatment. The 'I am an innocent survivor' affirmation can never be repeated too much. We need to go on our journey. Right now, it is just you and The Girl Next Door™ so let's get started.

CHAPTER ONE

It is Not Your Fault, Really

The Girl Next Door™ is fourteen years old. She lives in a two-bedroom apartment with a parent and two brothers. Her parent randomly invites men she meets into the apartment without telling her children.

The Girl Next Door™ walks to the kitchen. She has no make-up on and is fully clothed. She wants some water. She walks down the hall and enters the kitchen. She is surprised to see her parent lying on an area rug entertaining a strange man she has never seen before.

The parent stops her and briefly introduces her to the man. The Girl Next Door™ is cordial; however, the man has this ominous smile. She gets her water, returns to her room, and closes the door.

A few days later, the rotary dial telephone rings. The Girl Next Door™ answers the phone. It is the guy her parent introduced her to a few days prior. He graphically tells the sexual things he would like to do to her. He tells her not to tell anyone about the call. The Girl Next Door™ goes into her brother's room and tells them precisely what the man said he wanted to do to her. After all, they were nobody, so it was alright.

Without saying a word, her older brother storms out of the room. He goes to the parent and firmly states the man can never return to the apartment.

This was the first time a sexual assault was stopped. There are way too many more of these to come. Stay strong; we can get through this together.

In the space below, write about the first time you experienced unwanted sexual attention. How did you handle it?

CHAPTER TWO

Don't Blame Yourself

Like yourself, The Girl Next Door™ initially blamed herself. What if she hadn't left her room for a drink of water? Did she do something to lead him on? Was she somehow inappropriately dressed?

We always want to know why, and when we can't figure it out, we blame ourselves. Sometimes bad things happen to good people just as good things happen to bad people. Sometimes things are beyond your control. Never blame yourself.

You may have been a toddler, a child, a teenager, a young person, or even an adult. Adversity happens. It doesn't matter how you were dressed, what expression was on your face, or whether you were too kind or not. Life happens. There are good and bad people, and sometimes innocent people are affected.

To move forward, you must accept that you may have just been in the wrong place at the wrong time. Instead of blaming yourself, talk to someone.

Sometimes sexual assault victims get justice; the judicial system fails them other times. Take the risk. Be courageous. Get closure. If you keep it to yourself, you will internalize the trauma. The trauma will take various destructive forms.

As stated in the introduction, sexual assault is a lifetime trauma. You may remember how the human smelled or hear the sound of their voice, see their face reappear, or relive the experience repeatedly. You must be ready to have a solution when having a flashback.

Whether it is a relative or someone you should be able to trust, like a teacher, law enforcement officer, priest, pastor, or other religious people, get the strength to tell someone. You may not be believed. You may have to press legal charges. Stay strong. If you remain silent, others may be victimized.

Whatever you do, do not blame yourself. You are worthy of love and kindness. You are more than just an object of some person's lust. You are an innocent survivor. You will smile again.

CHAPTER THREE

I Made a Mistake; It's My fault

The Girl Next Door™ is fifteen. Like most girls this age, she is starting to get interested in the opposite sex. She dates a guy that is her friend's cousin. He is a hoodlum, but that is okay because he is her friend's cousin.

One day, she goes with her best friend to the mall. They stop in the arcade room. The Girl Next Door™ meets the cutest boy. He is one year older. He has flawless, smooth cocoa skin and sparkling brown hazel eyes. She watches him play video games. He asks for her telephone number so they can keep in touch. He has aspirations and comes from a nice family. His father owns a barbershop, and they live in a very swanky neighborhood.

The guy The Girl Next Door™ met at the mall had so much going for him. He adored her. They were young, but he wanted to marry her. She decided to break things off with her friend's cousin to be with him.

Unbeknownst to her, it was not that simple. The friend's cousin didn't want her to go. He threatened to harm her family if she left him. He agreed not to hurt her family on one condition; she allows him to see her one more time.

She meets him at the spot he requested. As soon as The Girl Next Door™ arrived, he lifted his shirt to expose a firearm in his waistband. She realizes she must comply. He states he would take her to his auntie's apartment to assault her sexually.

Under duress, they start walking. When they arrive at his auntie's apartment, to his surprise, his aunt was there. His plans were interrupted.

They leave his auntie's apartment as he walks her to the bus stop. Her mouth clenches tightly as he takes a kiss. That is their last encounter. Sure, The Girl Next Door™ made a mistake in dating him in the first place. She trusted him, and he betrayed her. She thought everything was her fault and learned not to be so trustworthy.

Release why you feel you were partially at fault for what happened to you below.

CHAPTER FOUR

Condemning Yourself

As if condemning yourself is not bad enough, society may blame you. Statements implying you sent mixed signals, should have known not to meet the offender alone or were you wearing any clothing to entice the perpetrator.

Your confidence and self-esteem have already taken a hit. Don't succumb to people who downplay the situation or blame you for what happened. You are an innocent survivor.

You may be blaming yourself as a coping mechanism. You must find other coping methods because blaming yourself does not promote healing.

It does not matter how you initially felt about the person. You cannot control how others behave. You may keep reliving things you could have done to stop the sexual assault. This is a waste of time because the person was stronger than you.

The fight or flight response only gives two reactions to stressful or threatening situations. A person can either fight to defend themselves; however, most times, the perpetrator is stronger or may have a weapon. The other option is flight, which means running away or escaping. Sometimes escaping is not possible.

When fight or flight is unavailable, a third response is to freeze. For thousands of years, freezing has been a survival mechanism used by mammals. Mammals will freeze to make themselves less attractive prey to predators by simply slumping to the ground to play dead.

When victims freeze during a sexual assault, they blame themselves for not doing enough to stop the attack. Unfortunately, outsiders often confuse freezing with consent. During a sexual assault, people freeze when they feel trapped and do not want to worsen the situation.

No one knows precisely how they will respond to a situation until they experience it themselves. The Girl Next Door™ has used all three, depending on the circumstances. Whether fight, flight, or freezing occurred during your situation, accept that you did the best you could under the conditions. After all, you are an innocent survivor.

CHAPTER FIVE

You Did the Best You Could at the Time

There are far too many sexual assaults that occur domestically via bad associations. Sometimes we make mistakes. We believe lies and must deal with the consequences. You may have been tricked, lied to, or deceived, which put you in a dangerous situation. It is okay. It is alright. You must forgive yourself and accept the consequences.

People are untruthful and deceptive, whether it is an acquaintance, a relative, or a best friend. Most sexual assaults are committed by people known to the victim. If you were tricked, do not blame yourself. You survived. Living with the consequences is complicated and ongoing, but you can do it.

CHAPTER SIX

Always Listen to Your Intuition

The Girl Next Door™ is nineteen. She stops by an ATM to get a small amount of cash. She feels danger. She looks around and sees three young men. Her intuition tells her to cancel the transaction and return to her vehicle. She ignores the red flags and proceeds with the transaction.

As the three guys got closer, her intuition became stronger to cancel the transaction and return to her car. She finally realizes she must listen to her intuition. She cancels the transaction. While waiting for her atm card to return from the machine, the three guys catch up to her. Two guys stayed on the sidewalk while one guy with a metal pipe approached her. He told her he would bust her head open with the pipe if she screamed or resisted. Fight, Flight or Freeze? The Girl Next Door™ was frozen as the guy touched her buttocks. Afterward, he walked over to the two other guys and left.

Notice he didn't try to rob her. He doesn't want money from the ATM. This is a perfect example of how sexual assault is not just about desire but power. The perpetrator has a need for dominance and control.

Be transparent with yourself. Write below about any inclination you had beforehand that you were in danger of being harmed before the situation happened.

CHAPTER SEVEN

You Have a Built-in Danger Warning System

You have an internal built-in warning system that allows you to know, even if it is only a few seconds beforehand, when danger is present, or something terrible will happen.

You must always adhere to this internal system. People, particularly women, ignore this internal system. Please do not ignore this preprogrammed internal system. If you are used to ignoring your intuition, stop it.

Make it a regular habit to always listen to your intuition, even if you are wrong. It is better to be incorrect, which may happen from time to time than to ignore your intuition and be sexually assaulted, a victim of crime, or something even worse.

You are a trinity, body, soul, and spirit. When you are spiritually not where you should be, your intuition may not be as sharp or keen. It is okay. It is alright. Follow your intuition anyway. If you are wrong, focus on strengthening yourself spiritually, and your intuition will improve. Keep working on yourself so that you trust your intuition and appreciate it, whether wrong or right.

CHAPTER EIGHT

You Cannot Trust Everyone

The Girl Next Door™ is now twenty-one years old. She works in a university's law school and accounting department to get through college. During the summers, she works as a supervisor in the payroll department for the city. She studied Spanish in high school but wasn't proficient. The payroll department she supervises is a Spanish-speaking community.

A guy who works in the building befriended The Girl Next Door™. He speaks Spanish and states he would teach her. He wants to meet her in a conference room in the building for lessons. The lesson is going well until he says, in Spanish, he loves her. From there, he tries to force a kiss. Things escalate quickly. This time, The Girl Next Door's™ response is to fight. She pushes a conference table and turns over some chairs. She makes it out of the room. She runs to the elevator. The elevator doors are closing. With one inch left before the doors closed, the guy reopened the elevator doors by sliding his hand into the opening.

The Girl Next Door™ knew she would lose, so she tried to talk her way out of it, and it worked. He believed her and allowed her to return to the floor where she worked, thinking they would be together some other time. She never saw him again.

In the space below, write about the person you trusted who betrayed you.

CHAPTER NINE

Be Careful Trusting People

Whether it is the single mother trusting a babysitter with her kids or a child trusting an authoritarian figure or a supposedly friendly neighbor, be cautious with the people you trust. Humans are imperfect, and that is enough reason for you to exercise caution with everyone, including your family members, neighborhoods, friends, and acquaintances. Remember, most sexual assaults are by someone the person knows.

You decide to get with some friends and go out to a comedy club or perhaps a birthday celebration or a graduation party. Refreshments are available. Constantly monitor your beverages. Never leave your table empty with your beverages while you go to the restroom. Unmonitored beverages may get spiked. Be overly cautious. Put a napkin over your drink, take it with you, or finish the glass before leaving the table. If you want to be extra careful, drink sealed bottled water or juice.

According to the Office on Women's Health, below are the three most common sexual assault drugs used:

- Rohypnol, known as Roach, Mind Erasers, and Roofies
- GHB, known as Cherry Meth, G-Juice, and Liquid Ecstasy
- Ketamine, known as Kit Kat, Special K, and Super Acid

Rohypnol is a potent sedative drug. It is a party drug that belongs to the drug class benzodiazepines. It causes the central nervous system to slow down. When ingested, it produces a slow reaction time, so you can't keep up will real-time events happening around you. It causes drowsiness and confusion, so you will not be fully aware during the sexual assault. It will be hard to remember details because it causes amnesia.

GHB (Gamma Hydroxybutyrate) is a psychoactive drug used in a medical setting as a general anesthetic. It was discontinued because of severe side effects. Now it is only used for the treatment of narcolepsy.

It slows down neurons in the brain and spinal cord. When used as a date rape drug, it produces unconsciousness and memory loss.

Ketamine is an anesthetic used in a medical setting by doctors as a drug used to induce loss of consciousness. It is used to spike drinks. It works quickly; innocent survivors will not have enough time to react after tasting bitterness in their drink. The innocent survivor loses consciousness very quickly, including muscle loss. It puts you in a dream-like state with amnesia, so you will not be able to remember the assault.

Sexual assault happens when you least expect it. It usually happens with someone you know and not just strangers. Always keep your guard up.

CHAPTER TEN

It Was Just a Date

The Girl Next Door™ is twenty-six years old. She has been married and divorced. People recommend that she go to clubs to meet a guy. She meets this guy at a club and agrees to go on a date with him.

The movie The Girl Next Door™ wanted to see was not showing in any movie theater, so they decided to go to the drive-in.

They agreed she would park nearby and get in his car for the movie.

He paid for their entrance and the concessions. The movie had barely started when he started to put his hands in between her thighs. She kept moving his hands. There was a misunderstanding. He was expecting sexual activity while she thought they were enjoying each other's company while watching a movie. She never saw the movie as she continuously moved his hands and told him no. The Girl Next Door™ realizes the situation could have quickly escalated to date sexual assault.

Afterward, she never returned any of his calls or went out with him again.

It is estimated that three out or four sexual assaults go unreported to the police, so the following statistical data is much higher.

(RAINN), Rape, Abuse & Incest National Network reports the following statistics related to perpetrators of sexual assault that show victims often know their attacker:

- 8 out of 10 sexual assaults are committed by someone the victim knows.
- 19.5% of sexual assaults are committed by a stranger to the victim.
- A victim's acquaintance commits 39% of sexual assaults.
- 33% of sexual assaults are committed by a current or former spouse, boyfriend, or girlfriend.

- More than one person commits 6% of sexual assaults

- A non-spouse relative commits 2.5% of sexual assaults.

Approximately 20% of women and 1% of men will experience date rape at some point in their lifetime. Again, it is imperative to always err on the side of caution, especially when meeting people on dating apps and social media.

Write about a time you went on a date or just went out and a perpetrator wanted to take advantage of you.

CHAPTER ELEVEN

Sexual Assaults on Dates

You consented to go on a date with someone, and their intentions were not pure. This is a date or acquaintance rape. The effects of this type of sexual assault are similar to stranger rape.

A significant difference between a stranger sexual assault and an acquaintance sexual assault is the innocent survivors usually blame themselves, never tell anyone what happened, and feel they caused their problem. They condemn themselves for being too nice or their clothing for being too provocative. If the date occurs in the evening, they criticize themselves for going out too late. The innocent survivors blame themselves for drinking if someone slipped something inappropriate in a drink. Most people encountering this situation feel self-humiliated and prefer to keep quiet about the situation.

In the date situation with The Girl Next Door™, outsiders would question why she agreed to go on a date to the drive-in movies with a guy she recently met at a club. It doesn't matter where you meet the individual. Whether you meet them online, at church, at a bar, or in some other social setting, anyone is capable of being an offender.

The innocent survivors that do report

what happened are often not believed. Sometimes they are even ridiculed and made fun of on social media. They are criticized for leading a person on to desire them sexually. This lack of support encourages innocent survivors to remain silent while the perpetrator goes on the assault more victims.

A proactive action to prevent date rape is always to be aware by not consuming intoxicating drinks. Dress modestly. Do not participate in any physical activity that could be misconstrued as consent. Please get to know the person mostly via talking to them over the telephone before you go out. Text messages do not count. Some people copy and paste text messages. You can also not pick up on tone over text messages; your intuition is extremely limited and disabled. Be prepared to defend yourself if necessary. Bear spray, pepper spray, a stun gun, taser, or concealed carry are possible options.

CHAPTER TWELVE

He Scared the Daylights Out of Me

The Girl Next Door™ is still twenty-six years old. After the incident at the drive-in, she takes a break from dating. She is a divorced single mother who wants to focus on being her best.

One day, she gets off work, picks up her daughter and returns to her townhouse. Shortly after entering the townhouse, the landline phone rings. She picks up the phone, and a creepy demented voice emerged. The man vividly describes sick, spine-chilling, and disgusting sexual things he wants to do to The Girl Next Door™. This call was before caller id technology was perfected.

The Girl Next Door™ tries unsuccessfully to use a code to trace the call. She calls the police; however, the police cannot pinpoint the person's exact location. The police determine the area the call came from. The call is from a co-worker at her job.

Without knowing exactly who made the call, The Girl Next Door™ is terrified. One day, a young man states The Girl Next Door™ is afraid without knowing anything about the telephone call. He says she should get a firearm. Realizing he is right. The Girl Next Door™ takes a class, buys a firearm, and eventually gets a concealed weapons permit.

Were you caught off guard by your sexual assault? Write about it below.

CHAPTER THIRTEEN

The Reality of the Situation

The reality of the situation is that people must be mindful of their surroundings. This includes being mindful of strangers, friends, acquaintances, co-workers, and even family members. It is always better to be overly cautious than to experience a sexual assault.

The Girl Next Door™ is cordial with most of her colleagues. She is a friend and a confidant. The employer she works for publishes a directory of all the employees, including their telephone numbers. Someone she extends kindness to; someone she trusts is demented and ready to take advantage of her.

This co-worker could have been someone in the maintenance department she talked to regularly and thanked for keeping her work area clean. It could have been someone on the security team that kept the workplace safe. It could have been someone in her same position or even a person in a higher position. She will never know, but whoever it is took advantage of getting her telephone number from the employee directory.

Fortunately, she only works for that employer for a year before moving on. She never has any closure; however, she does learn about the necessity of having a firearm.

Whatever method you decide is best for yourself to use as protection, be skillful with it and adequately trained.

CHAPTER FOURTEEN

Aftermath and Repeatedly Sexually Assaulted

When people experience childhood sexual abuse or sexual assault, it is a little-known

fact that they are at a much higher risk of being assaulted again in the future. The same is true once a person experiences domestic violence or robbery. For some reason, the innocent survivor is more likely to experience domestic violence or burglary a second time. This is sometimes called revictimization.

Studies have shown once a person is sexually assaulted, there is an increased risk of it happening again. The percentage of people sexually assaulted as children, adolescents, or adults is twice as high as those without an early sexual assault history.

Since sexual assault produces lifelong trauma. Multiple sexual assaults compound the trauma. Innocent survivors are more likely to suffer from post-traumatic stress disorder (PTSD), depression, eating disorders, self-harm, flashbacks, substance abuse, panic attacks, dissociation, and sleep disorders.

Self-care is essential for innocent

survivors. Utilizing more than one resource may be necessary to smile again. RAINN has a national sexual assault telephone hotline to assist you in this endeavor. Their telephone number is located at the end of this book. They provide confidential support from trained staff. They can help innocent survivors talk through what happened. They can give you a referral for long-term support in your area, information about the laws in your community, and local resources that can assist with your next steps towards healing and recovery.

The National Sexual Assault Hotline is a free safe, confidential service. They use only the first six digits of your telephone number or zip code to route your call. Your complete phone number is never stored. They will never release records or information about your call without your consent. Reports to the police or other agencies are only made when you consent, except when legally obligated. Most importantly, they have helped more than three million people with sexual violence.

Self-care also includes:

- Surrounding yourself with supportive people
- Learning to forgive yourself
- Being kind, gentle, and patient with yourself

Treat yourself to a scented bubble bath, some flowers, maybe a yoga class, or a new hairstyle.

Answering the prompts in this book will help you discover how you feel and give some release through writing. Talk about the situation with a professional. Learn about what other women have experienced. Take care of yourself by eating nutritious meals, doing the exercise of your choice, and getting some regular sleep.

Write a letter to the person or people who sexually assaulted you. This letter will not be seen by anyone other than yourself. Neither will it be sent.

CHAPTER FIFTEEN

Smiling Again

Let's revisit the question in the introduction. Can a human composed of a body, soul, and spirit overcome sexual assault? The answer is **YES**!

Even if a person takes every precaution possible, there is no guarantee they will not experience sexual assault. Read the optional bonus chapter to understand this better.

If you want to smile again, you have to forgive yourself, stop blaming yourself, be cautious, don't trust everyone, and try to learn a skill to use in case you don't want to respond with flight or freeze.

Lastly, always remember you have value and worth. You were created with a purpose in life. Continue to do the work to increase your self-esteem. Irrespective of what you have been through, never give up (that is another journey). Most importantly, always know that God loves you regardless of what happens during your lifetime.

For God so loved the world that He gave His only begotten Son, that whoever believes in Him should not perish but have everlasting life.
John 3:16 NKJV

Eternal life is a gift from God.

PERSONAL MESSAGE FROM THE GIRL NEXT DOOR™

Thank you for allowing me to go with you on your journey. This is such a heavy topic. I am sorry about what happened to you. This was a very challenging journey, but you made it. I hope I didn't disappoint you. If I didn't meet your expectations, remember I tried my best. I'm going back next door for now. Revisit this journey as often as needed. What is important is that you are a little better now. Keep taking things one day at a time. There are some blank pages at the end of this book for you to doodle, draw or write down any other thoughts about moving forward as an innocent survivor. It is time for me to go now; remember, I am just next door if you ever need me again.

About the Author

The Girl Next Door™, Mary Hendrix, is a retired professional educator. She earned a Bachelor of Science in Mathematics from UCLA and a Master of Arts in Theological Studies from Phoenix Bible College & Seminary. She is a trained pastoral counselor and hospice chaplain.

Mary has traveled the world, including all seven continents. She enjoys swimming, hiking, weightlifting, and cycling. Mary loves animals. She desires to help broken-hearted people live their best life.

You can contact The Girl Next Door™ at the following website and email:

mostbeautifulamongthousands.com

thegirlnextdoor@mostbeautifulamongthousands.com

National Sexual Assault Hotline

Available 24/7

1-800-656-4673

OPTIONAL BONUS CHAPTER:

You are not the only one.

There is nothing new under the sun. Some biblical characters experienced sexual assault. In this bonus chapter, we will examine a few women.

Trigger Warnings:

This bonus chapter mentions very alarming instances of incest, sexual assault, and gang rape. These women never had the opportunity to smile again. Skip this bonus chapter, if necessary.

TAMAR

II Samuel 13:1-19

Tamar was one of King David's beautiful virgin daughters. Her half-brother fell in love with her. He had such a crush on her that he became lovesick and lost a lot of weight.

The half-brother's adviser devised a scheme to lure Tamar into her half-brother's bedroom so he could sexually assault her. The advisor had the half-brother pretend to be ill, so he could ask his father to send Tamar to nurse him back to health by cooking for him.

King David sent his daughter to her half-brother's bedchamber to make food for him. While there, the half-brother raped her despite her pleading with him not to do it.

She was fully covered in modest clothing. She had on a long robe with sleeves. Tamar did nothing wrong as she was just making food for her supposedly sick half-brother at her father's request and ended up getting sexually assaulted.

After her half-brother sexually assaulted her, he hated her, put her out, and had the door locked behind her.

Then Amnon hated her exceedingly, so that the hatred with which he hated her was greater than the love with which he had loved her. And Amnon said to her, "Arise, be gone!"

So she said to him, "No, indeed! This evil of sending me away is worse than the other that you did to me." But he would not listen to her.

Now she had on a robe of many colors, for the king's virgin daughters wore such apparel. And his servant put her out and bolted the door behind her.

II Samuel 13:15-17 NKJV

Tamar put ashes on her head, which was customary in those times when someone died.

Tamar was a royal princess, according to her father's and mother's lineage. She was destined to marry a prince. After being sexually assaulted, she tears her robe, put her head in her hands, and cries bitterly. She is miserable, sad, and shamed for the rest of her life.

Tamar is a perfect example of an innocent survivor; except she ended up being a lonely woman who never smiled again. Nonetheless, God redeems even the desolate woman and will wipe every tear from her eyes.

DINAH

Genesis 34: 1-31

Dinah is the daughter of Leah and Jacob. A local prince sees her, abducts her, and sexually assaults her. Afterward, the prince wants to marry her. He is willing to pay a dowry and gifts. He even agrees to get circumcised. Dinah's brothers could not get over the rape. They retaliate by killing the prince and raiding the city.

CONCUBINE

Judges 19

A Levite has a concubine. The concubine ran away and is unfaithful to the Levite. She returns to her father's house. The Levite went to get his concubine. They stay with various people while traveling. They stayed with an older man when a mob of men came to the door. The men want to sexually assault the Levite. To spare himself, the man gives the mob his concubine. The mob sexually assaults her all night until she is deceased.

OPTIONAL BONUS CHAPTER:

Question & Answer Session for Christian Believers

The Girl Next Door™ has shared six potential sexual assault situations; therefore, she is in the statistical range to be revictimized. As a Christian, you may have asked the following questions, and The Girl Next Door™ will attempt to answer the questions.

Where was God when I was being sexually assaulted?

The Girl Next Door™:
God was there the entire time.

As believers, we know the Word of God is faithful. God inspires the scriptures. In Hebrews 13:5 God says, "I will never leave you or forsake you" NKJV. Furthermore, "I will never fail you. I will never abandon you" NLT. If God will never leave, fail, or abandon you, it means even in these sexual assault situations, He is there experiencing everything with you.

Why did God allow me to be sexually assaulted?

The Girl Next Door™:
God did not allow you to be sexually assaulted. On earth, good and evil exist together, so sometimes, experiencing bad things is unavoidable because when it rains, it rains on both the just and the unjust.

In the book of Matthew, chapter 13, Jesus uses parables to explain why good and bad people are currently intertwined on earth. Soon there will be a separation, but until then, even bad things can happen to good people.

The Parable of the Wheat and the Tares

Matthew 13: 24-30; 36-43

Another parable He put forth to them, saying: "The kingdom of heaven is like a man who sowed good seed in his field; but while men slept, his enemy came and sowed tares among the wheat and went his way. But when the grain had sprouted and produced a crop, then the tares also appeared. So the servants of the owner came and said to him, 'Sir, did you not sow good seed in your field? How then does it have tares?' He said to them, 'An enemy has done this.' The servants said to him, 'Do you want us then to go and gather them up?' But he said, 'No, lest while you gather up the tares you also uproot the wheat with them. Let both grow together until the harvest, and at the time of harvest I will say to the reapers, "First gather together the tares and bind them in bundles to burn them, but gather the wheat into my barn."

Then Jesus sent the multitude away and went into the house. And His disciples came to Him, saying, "Explain to us the parable of the tares of the field." He answered and said to them: "He who sows the good seed is the Son of Man. The field is the world, the good seeds are the sons of the kingdom, but the tares are the sons of the wicked *one.* The enemy who sowed them is the devil, the harvest is the end of the age, and the reapers are the angels. Therefore as the tares are gathered and burned in the fire, so it will be at the end of this age. The Son of Man will send out His angels, and they will gather out of His kingdom all things that offend, and those who practice lawlessness, and will cast them into the furnace of fire. There will be wailing and gnashing of teeth. Then the righteous will shine forth as the sun in the kingdom of their Father. He who has ears to hear, let him hear!

Why worship a God who allows horrible things?

The Girl Next Door™:
As believers, we walk by faith and not by sight. We continue to worship a God who allows horrible things to happen on earth because our reward will be so great in heaven that everything, we have experienced on earth will be worth it.

"Be happy about it! Be very glad! For a great reward awaits you in heaven. And remember, the ancient prophets were persecuted in the same way"
Matthew 5:12 NLT.

How am I supposed to forgive the perpetrator(s) who sexually assaulted me?

The Girl Next Door™:

Forgiveness is not for the wrongdoer; it is for the innocent survivor to be able to smile again. Even if the offender doesn't serve any jail time on earth, the offender will be judged by God for the evil done.

"But if you do not forgive men their trespasses, neither will your Father forgive your trespasses" Matthew 6:15 NKJV.

"When his case comes up for judgment, let him be pronounced guilty. Count his prayers as sins" Psalm 109:7 NLT.

I know so many people who have never experienced sexual assault. Why me?

The Girl Next Door™:
God will take every bad thing that has happened to us in our life, turn it into good, and use it for his purpose. Even when it seems our lives are falling apart, God is at work, and we have to trust that He will excellently use our experiences to help others.

"And we know that in all things God works for the good of those who love him, who have been called according to his purpose"

Romans 8:28 NKJV.

Why didn't he stop the attack if God loves me so much?

> The Girl Next Door™:
> During our stay on earth, God has given us free will to choose good or evil and life or death. People that choose evil and death are still given that right which means innocent survivors are impacted by their poor decisions.

"I call heaven and earth as witnesses today against you, that I have set before you life and death, blessing and cursing; therefore choose life, that both you and your descendants may live" Deuteronomy 30:19 NKJV.

Why didn't God help me when I asked?

The Girl Next Door™:
God did help you as you survived and made it through. He gives you peace.

"He calms the storm,
So that its waves are still"
Psalm 107:29 NKJV.

"Peace I leave with you, My peace I give to you; not as the world gives do I give to you. Let not your heart be troubled, neither let it be afraid" John 14:27 NKJV.

Made in the USA
Columbia, SC
21 June 2023

18539505R00057